W9-CDX-912

21st Century
Junior
Library

EARTH

by Charnan Simon

CHERRY LAKE PUBLISHING * ANN ARBOR, MICHIGAN

Published in the United States of America by Cherry Lake Publishing
Ann Arbor, Michigan
www.cherrylakepublishing.com

Content Adviser: Dr. Tobias Owen, University of Hawaii Institute for Astronomy

Photo Credits: Cover and page 4, ©Orlando Florin Rosu/Dreamstime.com; cover and page 8,
©Reistlin Magere/Shutterstock, Inc.; cover and page 12, ©Tim Martin/
Dreamstime.com; cover and pages 14, 16, 18, 20, ©NASA; page 6,
©Sebastian Kaulitzki/Shutterstock, Inc.; page 10, ©maryo/Shutterstock, Inc.

LIBRARY OF CONGRESS CATALOGING-IN-PUBLICATION DATA
Simon, Charnan.
 Earth/by Charnan Simon.
  p. cm.—(21st junior library)
Includes bibliographical references and index.
ISBN-13: 978-1-61080-081-5 (lib. bdg.)
ISBN-10: 1-61080-081-8 (lib. bdg.)
1. Earth—Juvenile literature. I. Title. II. Series.
QB631.4.S53 2011
525—dc22   2010052190

Cherry Lake Publishing would like to acknowledge the work of
The Partnership for 21st Century Skills.
Please visit www.21stcenturyskills.org *for more information.*

Printed in the United States of America
Corporate Graphics Inc.
July 2011
CLFA09

CONTENTS

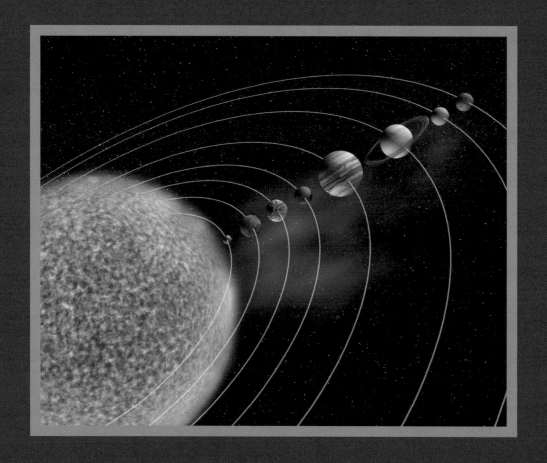

Each planet in the solar system moves around
the Sun.

Earth Is Our Home

Earth is one of the eight planets in our **solar system**. It travels around the Sun, just like all the other planets. But Earth is special. Earth is the only planet in the solar system where people, animals, and plants can live. Earth is our home!

The Sun is too bright to look at without special cameras.

Earth is the third planet from the Sun. If Earth were closer to the Sun, it would be too hot for us to live. If Earth were farther from the Sun, it would be too cold. Earth is not too hot or too cold. It is just right!

Ask Questions!

Earth is the fifth-largest planet. Ask your parents or teacher which four planets are larger than Earth. Which three planets are smaller than Earth? Asking questions is a good way to learn!

Earth's orbit is part of how we measure time.

Space Traveler

Like all the other planets, Earth travels around the Sun in a path called an **orbit**. Earth takes 365 days to go around the Sun. That's one year.

Earth speeds through space at almost 19 miles (31 kilometers) per second. That's fast! We can't feel this movement because we're moving right along with Earth.

Earth's axis is tilted just a little bit.

Earth moves in another way, too. It spins on its **axis**. Earth's axis is an imaginary line that runs through the middle of the planet. It goes from the North Pole to the South Pole. Earth takes 24 hours to spin all the way around on its axis. This makes one full day and night.

Create!

Roll some clay into a small ball. Poke a pencil all the way through the center. Imagine your clay ball is Earth and the pencil is its axis. Turn the pencil to make Earth spin on its axis!

A cloud is a collection of water droplets or ice crystals floating in Earth's atmosphere.

What on Earth?

Every planet in the solar system has a layer of **gases** surrounding it. This is called the **atmosphere**. Earth's atmosphere is made up mostly of **nitrogen** and **oxygen**. This is the air we breathe. Earth is the only planet that has the perfect mixture of air that people need to live.

Oceans cover most of Earth's surface.

Earth is also the only planet with a lot of flowing water on its surface. People need water to live. So do plants and animals.

Earth has rivers and lakes and oceans. It has plains and mountains and canyons. Earth has everything we need to live.

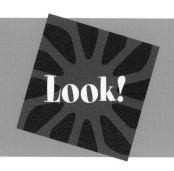

Look!

Water covers almost three-quarters of Earth's surface. From outer space, Earth looks blue because it has so much water. Sometimes Earth is called "the big blue marble." Can you see why?

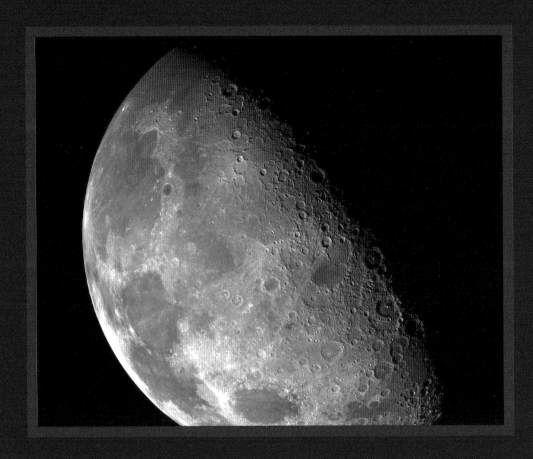

You can see the Moon in the sky on most nights, but sometimes you can only see it after midnight.

To the Moon and Beyond

Have you ever looked at the full Moon in the night sky? Almost all the planets in the solar system have moons. These moons circle around their planets while the planets circle around the Sun. Some planets have many moons. Earth has just one.

Neil Armstrong and Buzz Aldrin were the first astronauts to walk on the Moon.

The Moon is our closest neighbor in space. It is also the only place in space that people have visited.

Astronauts first landed on the Moon on July 20, 1969. **Scientists** are still studying the moon rocks and soil that the astronauts brought back.

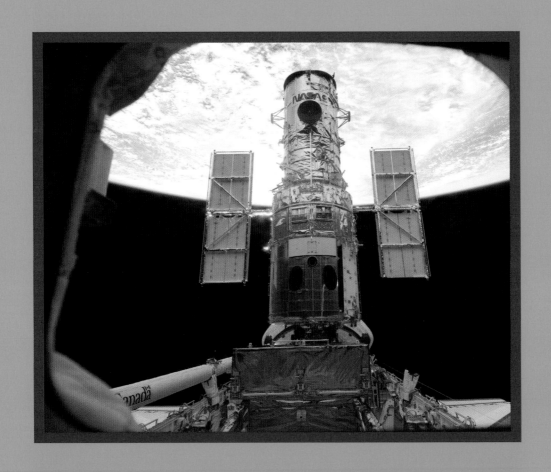

The Hubble Space Telescope helps scientists see far off into the universe.

Scientists use **telescopes** and spaceships to study other planets and stars in space. So far, they have not found any other place where people could live.

Earth is just one small planet in a huge **universe**. But it is just right for us!

Make a Guess!

Earth is the only planet in our solar system where people can live. Do you think people might be able to live on other planets outside our solar system?

GLOSSARY

astronauts (ASS-truh-nawts) people who fly in spaceships

atmosphere (AT-muhss-fihr) the gases or air surrounding a planet

axis (AK-siss) an imaginary line that goes through an object and around which the object turns

gases (GASS-ehz) substances, such as air, that will spread to fill any space they are in

nitrogen (NYE-truh-juhn) a colorless, odorless, tasteless gas that makes up about four-fifths of Earth's atmosphere

orbit (OR-bit) the path in which a planet or other object circles around another object

oxygen (OK-suh-juhn) a colorless, odorless, tasteless gas that makes up about one-fifth of Earth's atmosphere; humans can't live without oxygen to breathe

scientists (SYE-uhn-tists) people who study nature and make discoveries

solar system (SOH-lur SISS-tuhm) a star, such as the Sun, and all the planets and moons that move around it

telescopes (TEL-uh-skohps) tools used to look at faraway objects

universe (YOO-nuh-vurss) the planets, stars, and everything that exists in space

FIND OUT MORE

BOOKS

Chancellor, Deborah. *Planet Earth.* Boston: Kingfisher, 2006.

Wells, Robert E. *What's So Special about Planet Earth?* Morton Grove, IL: Albert Whitman & Co., 2009.

WEB SITES

NASA Space Place

spaceplace.nasa.gov/en/kids/ Enjoy games, projects, and fun facts about Earth and space.

Space.com—Our Solar System: Facts, Formation and Discovery

www.space.com/solarsystem/ Learn more about the objects in our solar system and how they were formed.

INDEX

ABOUT THE AUTHOR

Charnan Simon is a former editor of *Cricket, Click,* and *Spider* magazines. She has written more than 100 books for young readers and has lived on planet Earth her whole life.